Food For The Family Soul

Call Your Mother In-Law

Linda
Bring your
family to the table

Polly Wang

Copyright © 2019 Junk Food Kids LLC

ISBN 978-0-578-46166-3
eBook ISBN 978-0-578-46168-7

Cover Photograph Jon Northington
https://jlnphotostudio.smugmug.com/

Cover Editor Julia Rosher

Back Cover/Interior photographs
Ashley Nunez

Food For The Family Soul

Call Your Mother In-Law

Ashley Nunez

Thank you for buying this book. You are supporting the efforts of a mom and a family that has suffered through a lot of trial recipes. We are not a big publishing house. We are just a family. Thank you for supporting my dream!

I want to say thank you for the fantastic support I have received from my Husband Julian, my daughter Carmela, my son Julian and my dear friends Hunter Lightbourn and Karen Elizabeth Watts. Their support helped make my dream of this book possible

Table of Contents

Impress The Family

Stuffed Turkey Breast

Sunday Brisket
Brussel Sprout Gratin
Italian Chicken With White Wine Cream Sauce
Crab Stuffed Avocados
Halibut With Curried Cream Sauce

I Am Really Just Here For The Sides

Cauliflower Broccoli Bake

Lower Carb Cornbread
Spinach Salad With Warm Dressing
Oven Roasted Veggies
Bean Dip
Greek Village Salad

Warm Comfort

Broccoli Cauliflower Chowder

Nola Soup
Asian Noodle Soup
Creamy Chicken Tortilla Soup
Butternut Squash Curry Soup

Brunch My Favorite Meal

Low Carb Hash

Basic Breakfast
Pre-Work Out Breakfast or Snack
Spiced Sweet Potatoes with Smashed Egg
Banana Bread
Low Carb Pastries

You Had Me At Dessert

Whipped Tiramisu custard
Biscotti
Lemon Shortbread Cookies
Ricotta Cheese Cake
Mexican Spiced Chocolate Chip Cookies
Apple Crumble

Tasty Toppers

Almond Butter
Magic Green Sauce
Gremolata
Spicy Ketchup
Hunter's Sauce
Savory Almonds
Horseradish Compound Butter

Who Says They Don't Eat leftovers

Leftover Brisket Soup
Huevos Rancheros

Call Your Mother in law is the

Daughter in law edition of Food For The Family Soul, look at the bottom of each recipe to find out what you can call your Mother in law to make to compliment what you are cooking.

The beginning idea for this book came from my daughter, she asked if I would write half of my recipes in one cookbook for her and the other half in one for her future sister-in-law. The concept was born. Call your Mother in law is the first in a series of books Food For The Family Soul. Soon you will be able to bring your cookbooks together to create a fantastic meal. Ending all together around the table.

Many people have a family that is growing, Often times they do not know how to break the ice. My cookbooks are the catalyst to bring the family closer, bonding in the kitchen. The new daughter-in-law has received this cookbook from her mother-in-law, a reaching out to be part of the family. Now she breaks out her book to bring the family together, choosing to make the main dish, She calls her mother-in-law to make the complimentary side from another Food For The Family Soul book. Hopefully, her sister in law or brother-in-law is up to making another side. Don't forget mom she can join the fun and make dessert.

At the core, we all need our families to be successful. Finding ways to get to know one another or strengthen a relationship can be complicated. This book is the perfect catalyst for families. I have found this was the perfect door for me into building the relationships with the

9

family I have now. A book that brings families together is just what is needed in the world today.

2 years old and learning in the kitchen with my grandfather.

Biography

"I feel proud When Ashley cooks Cuban food but also love to eat her lasagna. The Italians and Cubans are alike we cook for others because we love."

Nena Nunez (my mother-in-law)
Kansas city star February 5, 2014

I grew up in a small Italian family. I was an only child born of an only child. So I spent my time with adults cooking in the kitchen for as long as I can remember. I learned a lot growing up, but I have my own style. I have taken some cooking classes here and there however I am self-taught. One of my earliest memories is standing on a stool in my great grandmothers (who spoke Italian) kitchen stirring a pot of sauce. Cooking is in my blood.

The life I have lived has led to this point. Cooking from the age of two, moving tons. (16 schools by the time I graduated from high school). At 11 I had a neighbor from Louisiana. I became her mother's helper, She introduced me to okra and gumbo, I found I loved southern food and wanted to know everything she would teach me. Every time we moved was an opportunity to meet new people and find exciting flavors. Growing up with an Italian upbringing and marrying into a Cuban family, I have melted my cooking into an eclectic style. Where I have

11

found my self during all these transitions is in the kitchen. Families come together in the kitchen what better way to get to know each other faster than by cooking and eating together. I met my husband over twenty years ago within months I was cooking dinner for my soon to be in-laws in their kitchen. Between my Italian upbringing, blending into my Cuban family, living on the west coast, west, midwest and the south, my cooking touches many people. People are always asking for my recipes. I work hard to get them just right. Nothing makes me happier than seeing my family love their food. My travels influence my food. I find it exciting eating my way through a destination.

As I have traveled through my life into motherhood, I have found that the best time in the kitchen now is with my own children. Now, teens, they experiment with their own recipes. Homemade birthday cakes have been made by my amazing daughter. We can during the summer, the pop of the lids is a big draw. My salsa is very popular. As I type this, I realize I need to get some canning done.

Life Changes

As I was writing this book my life took a sudden and drastic change. Our lives were turned upside down when my son became very ill. He was hospitalized and diagnosed with Type 1 Diabetes. This is life changing. We had to take classes about nutrition and learn to live with diabetes before we were released from the hospital. Instructors were impressed with our knowledge of food. I have been studying food for about 14 years, due to my daughters preservative allergies. Even with our understanding including medical that my family has, this was HUGE. FOUR days later our family had a sudden shock again. I went to the ER and diagnosed with Type 1 Diabetes as well. People are always shocked to hear our story. No family history, yet here we are. For all of those living with this disease, my heart and love are with you. This is a disease that is more challenging than people realize. It takes a lot of work with no days off. Managing diabetes and cooking for all the different eating styles, I have created recipes for a wide range of tastes. I am cooking for, preservative-free diet, some eat meat, and some don't, high fiber diet and low carb diet. So out of my family, this is just a few family members not mentioning the picky eaters and those who will eat anything. You will find something for everyone in this book. Because cooking for all the different diets and eating styles does not have to be complicated. I am finding ways to make life easy. I am eager to share my recipes with you and help your family eat healthy together.

I know many people try to keep within a diet lifestyle so I will have recipes noted with what diet they fall into. I eat a variety of styles maintaining a healthy diet with lots of fruit and vegetables in my day. There is something for everyone!

Homestyle This is just yum something grandma would make not caring about carbs or fat.

Mediterranean

focused on olive oil, legumes, fruit, vegetables, fish, cheese and yogurt.

Paleo

focused on nuts, fruit, vegetables, roots and meat (no dairy).

Keto

lots of grass-fed butter, cream, nuts, coconut oil eating low to no carb and high good fat.

I have been working hard to give nutritional information. Hopefully, this will help your family. Knowing carb counts is necessary information for Type 1 Diabetics. So become the favorite relative of your type 1 family member and give them a small menu of the carbs in the meal about to be served. Brownie points!! When we were at the children's hospital, we were recommended to use recipes.sparkpeople.com I have found that the carb counts have worked for both my son and me from the site. So I decided after talking to a food lab this was the best way for a self-publishing author to go. The only way to get the most accurate carb count is to make each recipe and have a chemical analysis done on each cooked item. Notice on some recipes carb counts do not include bread do to the fact that depending on the kind of bread carbs can vary considerably, and some people don't eat bread. Carbs can change if you deviate from the recipe, I am all for creativity, just keep this in mind if you are cooking for someone with T1D.

Look for Carb and protein counts at on each page.

Pantry

At our last diabetes class, we attended people asked me for some tips for making food every night. I thought I would share with you some of the tips I shared in class. First I keep some basics in the house at all times. Not all of these are used in the cookbook, they are all used on my Instagram and blog. I will preface with almost everything is organic in my house unless I can't find it organic or the organic version makes no difference. Go with the assumption that most are organic.

chicken soup base
chicken bone broth
Irish butter
local honey
coconut sugar
extra virgin olive oil
coconut oil
lemon juice

Frozen vegetables:
   green beans
   butternut squash
   cauliflower rice
   peas
Fresh fruit and vegetables
   riced cauliflower
   mushrooms
   onions
   garlic
   sweet peppers

asparagus
spinach
lettuce
carrots
tomatoes
kale
avocados
brussel sprouts
broccoli
apples
cherries
strawberries
grapes
blackberries
raspberries
pineapple (fresh and frozen).

The other tricks for always having food hot and ready, on busy nights are simple.

I have five crockpots. Three of mine are in a station for easy serving. They have a warm setting so I can cook and then just keep warm. Really helpful when people are coming over so you can get the clean up done before people arrive.

The timer on your over. I admit when I first started using the timer I was nervous. Would it really work? This is a life saver.

Prep ahead of time. Anytime you can plan ahead or prep some of the food, do it. Saving time is what we all want.

These simple things will help you get your family back to the table in no time.

Look for CHEAT recipes in the book for some that use some pre-made items.

T1D Tips

I was asked to put this in my book by a few fellow
T1Ds so as requested….
I get asked a lot about how I manage my T1D so
well. It is nothing magic. I go to my Dr
appointments and keep track of my A1C. I have
a continuous glucose monitor (CGM), this has
been a fantastic tool in keeping my sugars in
check. I eat in moderation. I eat small meals
during the day, 4 to 5. Some of these meals are
snack size. I eat a lot of vegetables and snack on
almonds and cheese. I work out five or more
days a week. Mostly Cardio with some light
weights and core exercises. I walk my dogs about
5 days a week, a mile and a half (as long as its
good weather). If I know I am going to be sitting
a lot during the day, I make sure I work out
before the day starts.
I drink a lot of water. I love this water that
comes in 25 oz bottles. I have always been a big
water drinker.
I admit I crave a sweet after I eat, to satisfy that
craving I eat 1 to 2 dark chocolate covered
almonds. I love these, and they feel like such a
treat.
I do splurge once a week and eat a higher carb
meal for me. When I do, I try to plan on an
additional workout. That way it's is easier to
manage any post high. Some carbs are really
hard on me, so I don't eat those at all (I don't eat
rice at all). I really try to stay away from the
foods that are hard on me. My splurge days are
usually on the weekend, like Sunday Brunch the
best meal of the week!! Always count your carbs.

I work closely with my doctor to continually adjust for my needs. Don't hesitate to ask for help from your doctor and educator.   JDRF has a lot of information, so reach out to them. When I find someone who is giving useful information or sharing great ideas, I will share them in my Instagram story. I really hope my knowledge can help others. A food journal can really help you figure out which foods you manage well and which ones you don't. Everyone is different, so you really have figure out what works for you. Snacking on almonds and avocados really help me avoid lows. Plain yogurt is another go to for me. I have found I really like working with coconut sugar and use this as my main sweeter when baking. My daughter did some research, she has been right, I do not get big sugar spikes from coconut sugar. I use small amounts, things do not need to be that sweet to taste good. Once you get used to less sweet food, you will be shocked at how much more you notice the other flavors in the recipe. Often times really sweet things don't taste as good to me anymore.

Social Media

Instagram
JUNKFOODKIDS

Facebook
JUNKFOODKIDS.COM

Greetings and Conversations

Deviled Eggs

Carbs 0.3g Protein 3.2g

Ok, I give! So many people have asked for these, I am adding them to the book. Really, this recipe is so easy. Use your favorite mayo, I can't tell you mine because of legal mumbo jumbo. But the one I like has a little zip to it. The serving size is for carb count, really you don't want to know how many people eat at my house. Serve them as an app or a side. No matter when you put them out they will be a hit.

Makes 24 Servings

12 eggs hard   boiled
3 tbsp mayonaise
2 tbsp dijon mustard
1 tsp dill dried
1 tbsp capers drained
Paprika optional

Directions

Peel hard-boiled eggs.
Slice each egg in half lengthwise.
Scoop yolks in a bowl and place whites on an egg plate.
Add Mayo, mustard, and dill to your yolks. I like to use the whisk on my electric mixer, you can mix by hand. Once all incorporated and creamy add capers and fold in so that they do not break apart. Scoop about a teaspoon of yolk mix into concave of each egg white. Sprinkle each egg with paprika. Chill in the refrigerator until ready to eat.

Food For The Family Soul
Call Your Mother in Law to make Mushroom burger sliders.

Spinach Artichoke Stuffed Mushrooms
GLUTEN-FREE * KETO * HOMESTYLE * NUT FREE

Carbs 2.4g Protein 2.2g

I love these as a side and an appetizer. I always make a couple of vegetables for dinners because I don't generally eat meat. And even when I do its usually a seafood or on occasion turkey. These are great leftovers for lunch with a salad. Unfortunately, we don't often have any leftovers.

Makes 18 Servings

18 baby bella
    mushrooms
1 Cup fresh spinach
1/2 package of cream
    cheese
1/4 cup chopped
    yellow onion
8 quarters of marinated
    artichoke hearts
2 tbsp grated parmesan
    cheese

Directions

preheat oven to 350

Clean and remove stems from mushroom caps. Line a baking sheet with parchment to place mushroom caps. Put remaining ingredients into a food processor. Pulse to process until you get a nice texture with some chunks of vegetables still remaining. Stuff spinach artichoke dip into each of your mushrooms. Place mushrooms in oven and bake for 8-10 minutes. You want the mushrooms to be firm. Serve warm.

Food For The Family Soul
Call Your Mother in Law to make almost any main dish.
This is so good as a part of any meal.

27

Cauliflower Italian Bread Sticks
GLUTEN FREE * KETO * NUT FREE

Carbs 6.4g Protein 5.2g

This is low-level carb comfort food. I love these so much I don't even miss bread and all those bad carbs, I can't eat anymore. This is so easy to make, you can make it any time of the week.

Makes 12 pieces

3 cups fresh riced cauliflower
2 cups shredded 6 cheese Italian blend
2 eggs
2 tsp Italian seasoning
1 tsp granulated garlic
1/4 cup shaved grana padano cheese

Directions
Preheat oven to 425
.
Reserve your Grana Padano cheese for the end.

In a medium bowl mix all other ingredients together. Place parchment paper on a half size sheet pan. Pour mixture onto parchment paper. Flatten and shape the batter into a rectangle. It should be about the size of a medium flatbread. Bake in the oven for 25 minutes or until golden. Top with Grana Padano cheese and place back in the oven just until the cheese melts. Let stand a few minutes before cutting.

Cut into 12 strips and serve with marinara or pizza sauce if you like to dip.

Food For The Family Soul
Call Your Mother in Law to make
Red Pepper Soup

Spinach Mushroom Quesadilla

Carb 4.0g Protein 4.9g

These are so popular I try to make them on taco Tuesday. For the recipe I will carb count with out the tortillas and you can just add the carbs of your brand to the count, You can really change the count on these if you can find a low carb tortilla.

Makes 8 pieces

1 tbsp olive oil
1/2 medium
   yellow onion
   sliced
10 oz portobello
   mushrooms
1 tsp chicken soup
   base
1/4 tsp ground
   cumin
1/8 Cayenne
   pepper
4 cups fresh
   spinach
4 medium tortillas
1 cup of shredded
   Mexican blend
   cheese

non- stick spray

Directions
In a medium skillet place olive oil and onions over med-low heat. Cook until onions become translucent. Add mushrooms and cook until they start to sweat. Add soup base cumin and pepper. Start stirring in spinach one handful at a time. Cook until liquid from vegetables has evaporated. Spray a piece of foil with non-stick spray and place a tortilla. Spread half of the mixture on Tortilla. Top with half of the cheese. Top with another tortilla. Spray a second piece of foil with nonstick spray. Place foil on top of quesadilla and wrap edges of both pieces together so that edges are sealed. Repeat with remaining ingredients.
   Place each foil wrapped quesadilla on a baking sheet. Place in a 350-degree oven for 5 to 8 minutes. Remove from oven.
   Unwrap quesadillas and cut into four pieces each.

Food For The Family Soul Call Your Mother in Law to make Fresh Salsa. Call your Brother to make Queso Dip

Kale Chips

GLUTEN FREE * KETO * MEDITERRANEAN * NUT FREE

Carbs 6.5g Protein 3.2g

My daughter loves these. If I know girls are coming over to study, I make these. Kale chips have a great crunch and are perfect satisfaction for the
vegetarians in your life.

Makes 4 Servings

(if you can keep to a serving size)
1 16 oz. bag of Fresh Kale
1/4 cup grated
   Parmesan and
   Romano cheese
   blend
3 tbsp olive oil
1 tbsp Lemon juice
1/8 tsp granulated garlic
1/8 tsp Cayenne powder

Directions

Preheat oven to 250

Wash and remove stems from kale leaves and discard stems. Place kale leaves to the side on paper towels and dry. Mix remaining ingredients. Toss kale with seasonings. Line a baking sheet with parchment paper. Place kale on a baking sheet in one layer. Use two baking sheets if you need more room so that leaves do not overlap. This helps keep them crispy. Bake for 40 to 50 minutes. Serve the same day.

Food For The Family Soul
Call Your Mother in Law to make snack nuts

Crab Dip

Carbs 3.7g Protein 12.1g

I was thinking of a fun dip to have on New Year's Eve. This turned out to be one of my new favorite dips, I will defiantly be making this for one of our family gatherings. Celery is my dipper of choice.

Makes 8 Servings

8 oz cream cheese
1 cup sour cream
2 tbsp lemon juice
3 tbsp Worcestershire sauce
1 tbsp dried chives
1 cup shredded cheddar and jack cheese
1/4 cup shaved grana padano
1 tsp hot sauce
1 tsp dijon mustard
3 cloves garlic cheese
8 oz cooked crab meat
1/4 tsp paprika

Directions

Preheat oven to 350 degrees.

In a bowl mix together cream cheese, sour cream, lemon juice, Worcestershire sauce, chives, cheese, hot sauce, and mustard. Grade or minced garlic and mix into cheese. Fold crab into the cheese. Once everything is mixed well, put into a baking dish. Sprinkle paprika evenly across the top of crab dip. Bake in the oven for 40 mins.

Serve with pita chips or for a low carb option, celery, and carrots.

Food For The Family Soul
Call Your Mother in Law to make baked Spaghetti Squash

Tequila Shrimp

Carbs 0.3g Protein 4.3g

Summer in a bite. Ole!! I love to make these as an apprizer or addition to taco night. During the summer I throw them on the grill, for an outdoor fiesta.

Makes 4 Servings

12 Shrimp deveined
    and peeled
2 tbsp white tequila
1 tbsp lime juice
Zest Of 1/2 lime
    (1 tsp)
1/2 tsp paprika
1/4 tsp cumin

Directions

Toss all ingredients in a bowl together and place in the refrigerator for 30 minutes or longer. I like to heat up a .grill pan on the stove top. You can just sauté in a skillet if you wish. Place each shrimp on the hot skillet and cook flipping once until pink all the way through. Serve right away.

Food For The Family Soul
Call Your Mother in Law to bring the chips and
Fresh Guacamole

Family Time At The Table

French Dip Sandwich

Carbs 7.8g Protein 64.9g

Busy school night? Got you covered. Perfect for new cooks and never have leftovers. I do this in my slow cooker.   I always use organic soups to stay away from preservatives. The CARBS on this are without the bread.

Just add your carbs if you choose to eat with bread.

Makes 4 Servings

1 can of organic
    french onion
    soup
1 tsp granulated garlic
1 tbsp Worcestershire
    sauce
1 tbsp chicken soup base
Salt and pepper to taste
2 pound chuck roast
1 medium sweet onion
    sliced

    Four hoagie rolls
      optional

Other bases could be
Portobello mushrooms
    or lettuce cups

Directions

Mix french onion soup, garlic, Worcestershire sauce, chicken soup base, and salt and pepper together in your crockpot. Place your chuck roast inside the crockpot and spoon sauce over meat. Place sliced onion on top and all around beef. Cook in the crock for 8 hours on low. Warm rolls, if bread is going to be used, and shred meat with a knife and fork. Using tongs place meat in rolls. Spoon sauce into small bowls for dipping. Enjoy!

Food For The Family Soul
Call Your Mother in law to make
Sautéed Mushrooms. Call Your Sister to make
Spicy Sweet potatoes

Five Spice Salmon

Carbs 3.6g Protein 22.1g

Who needs to go to a restaurant when you can make salmon this good. You will feel like a pro when your family is eating this.

Makes 2 Servings

4 tbsp soy sauce
1/2 tsp five spice
    seasoning
1 tsp Hoisin sauce
2 wild Salmon fillets 4 oz
    each

Directions

Mix soy sauce, five-spice seasoning, and hoisin sauce together. Place mixture in the base of a dish that is just large enough for your salmon to lay in. Place salmon flesh side down into shallow dish with sauce. Let this marinate for 15 minutes in the refrigerator. Place salmon on a foil-lined baking sheet skin side down. Broil about 5 1/2 inches from broiler. Broil for 10 to 12 minutes or until fish flakes easily with a fork.
If its summer you can grill it outdoors.

Call Your Mother In Law to make Hot and Sour soup. Call your Sister to make Cauliflower Fried Rice

Traditional chili

Carbs 23.8g Protein 29.5g

Each book has a chili recipe. Call the family and have a chili cook-off. I usually make a traditional chili and vegetarian chili. Don't Forget the Lower Carb Cornbread.

Makes 8 Servings

1.5 lbs extra lean ground beef
1 medium yellow onion chopped
2 cans chili beans drained and rinsed
1 cup water
1 can tomato sauce
1 can diced tomatoes and chilis
3 cloves minced garlic
2 1/2 tbsp chili powder
1 tbsp chipotle hot sauce
2 tsp oregano
1 tsp paprika
1 tsp salt
1/2 tsp cumin

Directions

Brown ground beef in a skillet. Drain fat off of beef reserving 1 tbsp in the meat. Add onion to beef. Sauté Beef and onions about five minutes until onions are translucent. Place ground beef and onions in slow cooker. Add the remaining ingredients. Stir.

Cook on low for 4 hours or you can leave it longer if you are busy. Eat when you are ready

In each of the Food For The Family Soul you will find a variation of chili. So get ready to get together and have a chili cook off.

Low Carb Shrimp Jambalaya

Carbs 16.2g Protein 15.2g

I enjoy this as an alternative to the traditional Jambalaya with rice. I have this listed as a main that is great for a busy weeknight. Jambalaya has the ability to be served as a side if used as a side will make 6 to 8 servings.

Makes 4 Servings

1 tbsp butter
1 medium onion
    chopped
2 celery stalks chopped
1 yellow pepper chopped
1 tbsp tomato paste
3 cloves garlic pealed
    and chopped
2 Italian sausages
    cooked and sliced
1 cup tomato sauce
1 tbsp chicken soup base
1 tbsp chipotle hot sauce
1 tsp thyme
2 bay leaves
2 cups cauliflower rice
16 shrimp peeled and
deveined

Directions

Melt butter in large sauté pan add chopped vegetables and sauté until onions are soft. Add sausage and let the slices brown slightly. Add remaining ingredients, reserving the cauliflower rice and shrimp. Mix ingredients entirely and simmer for five minutes. Stir in Cauliflower one cup at a time. Simmer an additional 5 minutes. Add shrimp to pan cook until shrimp is pink. Serve and enjoy.

Food For The Family Soul
Call Your Mother in Law to make Ricotta Panna
Cotta with Blackberries
Call Your Sister to make
Pan Seared Fillet Mignon

Sloppy Joes

Carbs 19.4g Protein 21.8g

I am leaving the bread out of the carb count for this. If you
want to eat this low carb, you can use lettuce cups or large
portobello mushrooms as your base. And if you are all
homestyle or have a mixed group, offer some hoagie rolls.

Makes 4 Servings

2 lbs. ground beef or
    turkey
1 cup sweet red and
    yellow pepper,
    chopped
1 cup medium red onion
    chopped
1 can tomato sauce
1 tbsp horseradish
    mustard
1 tbsp coconut sugar
1 tbsp tomato paste
1 tsp granulated garlic
salt and pepper

Directions

Brown beef in a skillet. Drain
excess fat. Add chopped
peppers and onions. Sauté with
meat until peppers and onions
are soft. Add remaining
ingredients and let simmer on
low for 15 minutes, stirring
often. Top your favorite base
with sloppy joe mix. Mine is a
grilled portobello mushroom.

*Food For The Family Soul
Call Your Mother in law to make Broccoli Cheese
Soup. Call Your Sister to make Mexican Spiced
Chocolate Truffles*

Uncle Bob's Meatballs

HOMESTYLE * NUT FREE * PALEO

Carbs 10.6g Protein 25.1g

These are a favorite with my kids. They are affectionately called Bob's Balls. Keep it clean; this is a family cookbook. He is specific about the order each ingredient is mixed.

Makes 6 Servings

1/2 green pepper
1/2 medium yellow onion
1/4 of a bunch of fresh parsley
1 1/2 lb ground beef
3 eggs
1 tbsp oregano
2 tsp Italian seasoning
2 tsp salt
1/2 tsp crushed red pepper
1 1/2 tbsp minced Garlic
1/2 cup Italian bread crumbs

Directions

Preheat oven to 350 degrees. Remove stem and seeds of green pepper. Mince green pepper and onion. Remove stems from parsley and chop. Mix meat, peppers, onion, and parsley together. Whisk eggs together with oregano, Italian seasoning, salt, crushed red pepper, and garlic. Mix egg mixture and meat mixture. Add Bread crumbs and mix. Once mixed make into balls. I like using my cookie scoop so that the carb count is the same for each ball. Bake meatballs on a baking sheet in the oven until cooked through, about 10 to 15 minutes.
Serve with sauce of your choice.

Food For The Family Soul
Call Your Mother In Law to make Sautéed yellow Squash.
Call Your Sister to make Romesco Sauce.

Lemon Piccata Sheet Pan Dinner
GLUTEN FREE * HOMESTYLE * NUT FREE * PALEO

Carbs 40.7g Protein 18.3g

Sheet pan dinners are easy. You can get the family to the table and still manage to get other things done. I love the flavor of lemon in this dish, like a bit of warm summer.

Makes 4 Servings

4 chicken breasts
2 tbsp butter
1 tsp lemon juice
1 tsp turmeric
1 tsp granulated garlic
1 lb fingerling
    potatoes
16 brussel sprouts
1 tbsp lemon juice
1 tbsp olive oil
1 tsp oregano
1 tbsp white wine
salt and pepper to
    taste
4 Slices of lemon

Directions

Preheat oven to 350 degrees

Make sure your chicken breasts are trimmed of fat. Melt Butter and mix 1 tsp lemon juice, turmeric, and garlic together for the marinade and baste each chicken breast with marinade. Place Chicken breasts on a baking sheet. Clean Potatoes and trim any if needed. Cut brussels sprouts lengthwise in half. Whisk 1 tbsp lemon juice, olive oil, white wine, and oregano together. Toss potatoes and Brussel sprouts along with the sauce. Arrange vegetables in a single layer, around the chicken on a sheet pan. Top each piece of chicken with a lemon slice. Bake in the oven for 30 minutes until chicken is cooked through.

Food For The Family Soul
Call Your Mother In Law to make Mini Texas Cakes Call
Your Brother to make Spring Pecan Salad

Cuban Steaks

GLUTEN FREE * HOMESTYLE * KETO * NUT FREE * PALEO

Carbs 3.5g Protein 22.5g

I learned this recipe from my mother In-Law who now claims I make them better than her. But really I don't think I have changed anything from what she taught me. These are quick and easy to make. My family loves them. You can make them for a few people or a crowd.

Makes 4 servings

1 lb. thin cut steaks
    from a rump
    roast
Salt
pepper
1 tbsp olive oil
1 yellow onion
1 tbsp organic lemon
    juice

Directions

Your steaks should be cut breakfast steak thickness... I have the butcher cut my steaks, so they come out even and saves me time. Take each steak and sprinkle with salt and pepper. Turn steak over and repeat. Complete this process with each steak.
Heat olive oil in a skillet, place steaks one at a time in the skillet and brown both sides. When this is complete remove steaks and place on a plate. Keep in your oven on warm or in a warming drawer. Slice onions into thin strips. Add small sliced onions to the skillet and sauté when they are almost cooked through add lemon juice and deglaze the bottom of the skillet, pour liquid and onions over steaks and serve.

Food For The Family Soul
Call Your Mother In Law to make Aunt Gladys' Black Beans
Call your Sister to make Simple Avocado.

Zesty Chicken Drumsticks

Carbs 5.2g Protein 2.4g

These are quick and will have the kids and your hubby running for the table. I love simple recipes for busy nights. And I won't lie I love things that I can put in the oven. The oven is like the robot vacuums they work for me while I get other things done.

Makes 4 servings

2 lbs chicken drumsticks
1/4 cup horseradish
    compound
    butter, melted
    Page 140
3 tbsp pub style
    horseradish
garnish with fresh Thyme
    (optional)

Directions

Put drumsticks in a one-gallon plastic bag. Pour compound butter over chicken. Move the chicken around and make sure each piece is coated with butter. Seal plastic bag and place in refrigerator overnight.
Preheat oven to 425. Place chicken on a baking sheet.
Take a basting brush and brush each piece of chicken with horseradish. Place chicken in the oven. Turn over each piece after 20 mins. Bake another 20 minutes. Make sure drumsticks are cooked through and at 165 degrees with a meat thermometer.

Food For The Family Soul
Call Your Mother In Law to make Potato and Leak Soup
Call Your Brother to make Strawberry Trifle

Impress The Family

Stuffed Turkey Breast

GLUTEN FREE * HOMESTYLE * KETO * NUT FREE

Carbs 2.1g Protein 16.3g

This recipe is straightforward. Feeds a lot of people and will impress everyone. When you add sides, you have your full holiday meal. Great holiday centerpiece!

Makes 10 Servings

3 lb. fresh boneless
    turkey breast.
1 lb mild Italian sausage
    with out casing
2 tbsp salted butter
1 tbsp chicken soup base
1/2 tsp granulated garlic
1/2 tsp of dried thyme
1/4 tsp turmeric
1/4 tsp paprika
1 tbsp dried onion flakes

cooking twine

Directions

pre-heat over 400 degrees
Take your turkey breast and unroll skin side down. Take the sausage and spread evenly on top of the turkey. Depending on the size of the breast some times I can not get all the sausage to fit, that is ok. Now roll the turkey breast with the sausage inside, like a jelly roll. Wrap with cooking twine and tie tightly. Melt butter and mix the remainder of the ingredients together. Cover the outside of the turkey breast with seasoned butter. Place turkey in a baking dish and roast for 12 to 15 minutes per pound until internal temperature reaches 165. Let rest 10 minutes. Cut kitchen twine off and slice turkey. Place turkey slices on a platter and pour juices from baking dish over turkey.

Food For The Family Soul
Call Your Mother in Law to make roasted brussels sprouts. Call Your Sister to make Crab Dressing.

Sunday Brisket

Carbs 5.7g Protein 68.1g

Brisket is a great slow cook dish. Leave it in the oven and let it cook for hours while you run to church and hang out with your family. Come home later, and it feeds a crowd. Check this out!! This recipe comes with a leftover companion.

Makes 8 Servings

4 lbs. flat cut brisket
1 large onion
8 cloves of garlic
2 tbsp horseradish
    mustard
2 tbsp Worcestershire
    sauce
2 tsp pepper
1 tsp salt
1/4 tsp cayenne
    pepper
1/4 white wine
1 tsp beef soup base

Directions

Set aside brisket and onion. Mix remaining ingredients in a bowl. Place brisket in a dish and cover with your mix. Make sure you cover all sides of your brisket. Place brisket in the refrigerator and let marinade for at least one hour. Sometimes I let sit overnight. Slice onions. Place onions at the bottom of a dutch oven. Place brisket in dutch oven fat side up. Pour remaining marinade on top. Cover dutch oven with foil and place in an oven at 250 degrees. Set your timer and let cook for 5 to 6 hours. Until meat falls apart with a fork. I often cook this in the crock pot all day. I love anything I can put in the crockpot. Enjoy the rest of your day.

Food For The Family Soul
Call Your Mother in Law to make Broccoli Parm   Call Your Brother to make Black Bean And Sausage Soup

Brussel Sprout Gratin

Carbs 11.4g Protein 14.4g

Ready for compliments? Make this and let them flow, You will impress even the most reluctant veggie lover.

Makes 8 Servings

6oz Prosciutto
2 lbs brussel sprouts
1 tbsp thyme dried
1 tsp salt
3 cloves garlic minced
1/2 tsp ground black
    pepper
4 tbsp butter melted
1/4 medium yellow
    onion chopped
2 cups heavy cream
1 tbsp Dijon mustard
1/4 tsp cayenne pepper
1 cup Grana Padano
    shaved

Directions

Place prosciutto on a baking sheet in a single layer and place in the oven at 475. Cook, flipping once until crispy. Put prosciutto in a bowl and set aside. Reserve baking sheet. Trim and half Brussel sprouts. Toss Brussels sprouts with thyme, salt, garlic, black pepper, butter, and onion. Spread mix out on the previously used baking sheet. Roast brussels sprouts in the oven for about 15 minutes. Tossing often to make sure they cook evenly. Whisk heavy cream, dijon mustard, and Cayenne pepper together. Rough chop prosciutto. In an 8 x 11 baking dish place brussels sprouts mixture and prosciutto, toss together. Pour Cream mixture into baking dish. Top with Grana Padano spread evenly. Bake in the oven at 350 until the cream has thickened, bubbly.

Food For The Family Soul
Call Your Mother in Law to make Meat Loaf. Call your sister to make stuffed onions.

Italian Chicken With White Wine Cream Sauce

Carbs 10.5g Protein 17.3g

This chicken dish can be doubled for a crowd. I love to serve this, the chicken comes out fancy as if I have been working all day. No one will have any idea how easy it was to prepare.

Makes 4 servings

4 chicken breasts
2 tsp Italian seasoning
4 tbsp shaved Grana
    Padano cheese

Cream sauce

1/2 cup heavy whipping
    cream
1 tbsp butter
2 tbsp granda pandano
    cheese
2 tbsp white wine

salt and pepper to taste

Directions

Line a baking sheet with parchment paper and preheat oven to 350 degrees. Season each chicken breast with salt and pepper. Sprinkle each side of chicken breast with 1/2 tsp of Italian seasoning and 1 tbsp of Grana Padano cheese. Place each chicken breast on the parchment lined baking sheet. Bake in the oven for 20 mins or until chicken is no longer pink and internal temperature is 165 degrees. In a small saucepan add sauce ingredients. Whisk together over medium heat until all of your cheese melts. About 5 minutes. Place chicken on a plate when done cooking and pour cream sauce on top. Everyone will think you worked so hard.

Food For The Family Soul
Call Your Mother in Law to make Cuban Inspired Cauliflower. Call your sister to make Almond Green Beans

Crab Stuffed Avocados

GLUTEN FREE * KETO * NUT FREE * PALEO

Carbs 50.3g Protein 6.4g

I love crab cakes and avocados. I am incorporating both in a lighter version. These make a quick lunch or a beautiful side with dinner. Definitely would impress friends if you make a couple for a luncheon and serve with a bed of baby greens.

Makes 2 serving

8 oz cooked crab meat
2 tbsp organic butter
1/2 cup of chopped red
   onions
6 sun-dried tomato
   halves chopped
6 quarters of marinated
   artichoke chopped
4 cloves of garlic
1/2 tsp dill dried
6 tbsp organic sour
   cream
1 tsp of lemon juice
dash of Cayenne pepper
1/4 tsp dry mustard
2 Avocado
salt to taste

Directions

Drain crab meat and check for shell pieces. Put to the side. In a small sauté pan, on med-low heat, place butter and onions once onions begin to turn translucent add sun-dried tomatoes and artichokes. Let this sauté a few minutes so the ingredients mary a bit. Take two cloves of garlic and puree in a small mixer. Mince remaining cloves of garlic. Take your pureed garlic and add dill, sour cream and 1/4 tsp of lemon juice, whisk together. The sour cream mixture will be the sauce you drizzle on top. Add a dash or so of salt.
Add remaining garlic, crab, cayenne pepper, mustard, and lemon juice to your sauté pan. Mix and make sure it is evenly heated. About 4 minutes, Add salt to taste. Let cool slightly. Cut avocado in half, remove pit and skin. Place each half on a plate and fill the concave of avocado with your crab cake mixture. Drizzle with sour cream sauce and serve.

Food For The Family Soul
Call Your Mother in Law to
make Greek Salad.

Halibut With Curried Cream Sauce

GLUTEN FREE * HOMESTYLE * KETO * NUT FREE *
PALEO

Carbs 7.0g Protein 25.4g

This halibut is so good it would only be better if someone served it to me by the pool. I feel like I am on vacation every time I eat this light fish and sauce that makes me want to lick the dish.

Makes 4 Servings

4 fillets wild caught
    halibut
1 tsp curry
salt to taste

1 tbsp olive oil
1 tbsp butter
1/2 yellow onion
    chopped
1 carrot chopped
1 celery stalk
1/2 tsp curry
2 pinches saffron
1/4 cup white wine
3/4 cup chicken bone
    broth
3 cups fresh spinach
1 1/4 cup heavy cream

Directions

Season each fish fillet with curry and salt evenly. Heat olive oil in a frying pan. Place each piece of fish in the hot oil and sear each fillet 3 to 4 minutes on each side. Fish should be cook through so that it flakes.
Melt butter in a small soup pot. Chop onion, carrot, and celery. Sauté chopped vegetables in butter until soft. Add curry, saffron, white wine, and chicken bone both, Bring to a simmer, stir in spinach and reduce. Add cream. Serve warm sauce with vegetables at the bottom of the bowl and top with a beautiful halibut fillet. Enjoy.

Food For The Family Soul
Call Your Mother in Law to make Caesar Brussel Sprouts.

I Am Really Just Here For The Sides

Cauliflower Broccoli Bake
HOMESTYLE * KETO * NUT FREE

Carbs 8.3g Protein 5.1g

I love this recipe; It came about one night before Christmas. We were leaving for an extended family trip for Christmas; I still wanted to have a Christmas dinner at my house even though we were all going to be together. I was making the meal and trying to use up all the food I had left in the house. I contrived this at the last minute, and everyone loved it. Now it's an easy comfort food staple.

Makes 8 Servings

4 cups riced cauliflower
3 cups diced broccoli
15oz jar four cheese
   Alfredo sauce
1/4 cup white wine
1/2 tsp granulated garlic
1/2 cup grated
   parmesan
Salt and pepper to taste

DIRECTIONS

preheat oven to 350
Mix all ingredients in a bowl. Transfer to a 8 x 8 baking dish and bake until bubbly about 30 to 40 minutes.

Food For The Family Soul
Call Your Mother in Law to make Crab Stuffed Chicken.

Lower Carb Cornbread

Carbs 24g Protein 4.5g

I love this cornbread it has all the flavor of a regular cornbread without the sugar spike. Many regular cornbreads have a carb count of 38 my version knocks it down to 18. My family loves to put a slice of cornbread at the bottom of a bowl and top with hot chili. Leftovers are great warm with butter and a side of eggs.

Makes 9 Servings

1 cup almond meal
1 cup yellow cornmeal
1 scoop unflavored
    protein (serving)
3 1/2 tsp baking powder
1/3 cup raw honey
1 egg
1 cup unsweetened
    original almond
    milk
Pat of butter for greasing
    baking dish

Directions

Preheat oven 350 degrees. Grease 8 x 8 baking dish with butter.
Mix dry ingredients together until combined. In a separate bowl mix wet ingredients. Add dry ingredients to wet ingredients, mixing until combined. Pour into the baking dish and bake about 20 to 25 minutes, until the top starts to turn golden and a toothpick comes out clean. Serve warm with butter or with chili.

Each Food For The Family Soul cookbook there is a chili recipe. Make the cornbread and the chili in this book and call the family to make some chili for a family chili cook off!

Spinach Salad With Warm Dressing

GLUTEN FREE * HOMESTYLE * KETO * PALEO

Carbs 4.9g Protein 9.2g

When I was a little girl, my grandfather made me a salad with a warm dressing. I always use to look forward to going to his house just so he would make me the salad. This is my version of my childhood memory.

Makes 4 Servings

8 oz. baby spinach
2 large hard boiled
    eggs
5 slices procuitto
1/2 small red onion
    sliced thin
3 tbsp white wine
3 tbsp balsamic vinegar
1/2 tsp Dijon mustard
3 tbsp olive oil

Directions

Place spinach on a platter. Slice eggs and arrange on a bed of spinach. Cook prosciutto in a pan until crispy. Place prosciutto on paper towel. Deglaze pan with white wine. And add onions sauté until soft. Remove from heat. Place in a small saucepan. Add remaining ingredients and warm for a couple of minutes. Serve on salad while still warm. Eat right away.

Food For The Family Soul
Call Your Mother In Law to make Picadillo. Call you Sister in Law to make Black Beans.

Oven Roasted Veggies

GLUTEN FREE * KETO * MEDITERRANEAN * NUT FREE * PALEO

Carbs 10.1g Protein 2.0g

This is so easy you will probably throw this into regular rotation. I love the leftovers on a salad the next day. This is a really great recipe to have a new cook make while hanging out with you in the kitchen.

Makes 6 Servings

16 Brussels sprouts
3 carrots
1 large onion
1 large red pepper
10 cherry tomatoes
3 tbsp olive oil
2 tbsp white wine
   vinegar
1 tsp dijon mustard
Salt and Pepper to
   taste

Directions

Trim and half brussels sprouts. Peel and cut carrots into 2-inch sections. Slice onions into strips. Trim and deseed the pepper. Slice pepper into strips. Toss vegetables with remaining ingredients. Spread out vegetables on a baking sheet. Roast vegetables in a preheated oven at 475 degrees. Toss vegetables about every five minutes and roast for about 20 minutes.

Food For The Family Soul
Call Your Mother In Law to make
slow cooked pork roast.

Bean Dip

Carbs 23.4g Protein 9.3g

This is a super easy recipe. Grab the kids they can make this one. We eat this every time we have taco Tuesday. I make a double batch, so there are leftovers for breakfast check out who says they don't eat leftovers for the recipe.

Makes 4 servings

1 can refried beans
1/4 cup organic sour
    cream
1/4 cup shredded cheese
    Mexican   blend
1/4 cup favorite salsa

Directions

Put all ingredients into a medium pot. Heat on the stove top over medium heat. Stir occasionally until everything is incorporated and heated through. You should no longer see any bits of cheese. Server this with taco night. Great on tacos, nachos, and burritos. Everything is good with bean dip.

Food For The Family Soul
Call Your Mother In Law to make Creamy Chicken
Burrito. Call your brother to make Guacamole.

Greek Village Salad

Carbs 5.8g Protein 2.2g

One of the fastest dishes in the kitchen. I have been making it for many years, my husband loves it. One night a friend from Greece was over and said in Greece they call it village salad. So now it has a proper name.

Makes 4 servings	Directions
10 oz grape tomatoes 1 cucumber 1/4 cup feta cheese 1 tbsp olive oil 1 tbsp white wine vinegar Salt and pepper to taste	Cut tomatoes in half. Peel cucumber and cube into bite-size pieces. Mix all ingredients together in a bowl. You can serve right away. I think it is better if the flavors marry in the refrigerator for 30 minutes before serving.

Food For The Family Soul
Call Your Mother In Law to make Chicken
Skewers. Call your brother to make Greek Potatoes.

Warm Comfort

Broccoli Cauliflower Chowder

Carbs 10.5g Protein 19.4g

All the satisfaction of a more substantial soup. You can make it more luxurious with half and half instead of almond milk or keep it low carb and lower fat. With all the creamy cheese you won't miss the half and half.

Makes 6 Servings

1 tbsp extra virgin olive oil
1 medium yellow onion chopped
2 celery stalks chopped
4 1/2 cups riced cauliflower
2 cups chicken bone broth
1 tbsp granulated garlic
1 tsp ground turmeric
1/2 tsp paprika
3 cups raw broccoli
2 tbsp hot sauce
2 cups almond milk original unsweetened
2 cups shredded four cheese Mexican blend

Directions

Place olive oil in a stockpot over medium heat. Sauté onion and celery until onions are translucent. Stir in cauliflower, chicken bone broth, and spices. Bring to a simmer. Chop broccoli into bite-size pieces and stir into soup. Simmer until broccoli becomes dark green. About 3 to 5 minutes. Add almond milk, cheese and hot sauce stir until cheese is incorporated into the soup. Serve and enjoy!!

Food For The Family Soul
Call Your Mother in Law to make Chicken Caprese Sliders. Call Your Sister to make Protein Brownies.

Nola Soup

Carbs 12.3g Protein 15.1g

I was reading about the history of green gumbo one day. Its a traditional recipe made during lent in NOLA. That idea inspired this soup, now on regular rotation in my house. It has become my favorite soup, somehow it is like a memory of summer vacation, and all the food of the french quarter ladled in a bowl.

Makes 8 Servings

4 tbsp butter
1/2 large yellow onion
4 celery stalks
4 sweet red and yellow peppers
2 garlic cloves
1/2 cup white wine
2 bay leaves
12 fresh Brussels sprouts
4 cups of water
3 tbsp chicken soup base
1 tbsp lemon juice
1 tbsp Worcestershire sauce
1 tbsp hot sauce
2 cups broccoli chopped
4 cups fresh spinach
24 uncooked shrimp peeled and tail-off

Directions

Place butter in a stock pot and melt. Chop onion and celery sauté until onion is soft. Chop peppers and garlic, add to the pot. Add white wine and bay leaves, bring to a simmer. Trim and cut brussels sprouts in half and lengthwise. Add water, soup base, lemon juice, Worcestershire sauce, and hot sauce. Bring to a simmer. Chop broccoli into bite-size pieces and add along with the spinach and shrimp. Simmer until shrimp are all pink. Serve hot.

Food For The Family Soul
Call Your Mother in Law to make
Muffuletta
Call Your Brother to make Semifreddo

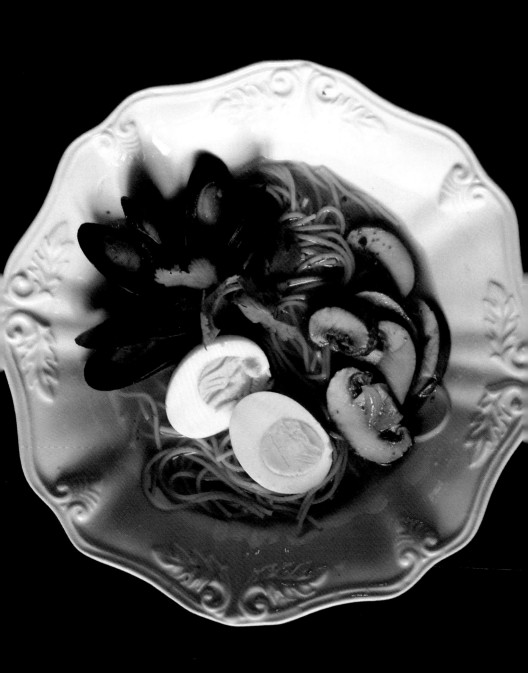

Asian Noodle Soup
(aka leftover noodle soup)

Carbs 39.9g Protein 6.1g

Really this soup was a bit of an experiment. I had some leftover spaghetti, and I had been wanting to try my hand at soba or ramen-type soup. I wanted something simple yet comforting. My kids love soup, and I love it when they are happy eating.

Makes 4 Servings

1 Tbsp butter
1/4 of a yellow onion
4 portobello mushrooms
1 lb frozen mussels in
    garlic and butter
4 cup water
2 tbsp chicken soup
    base
4 hard boiled eggs
1 inch fresh ginger
1 tbsp soy sauce
1 tbsp lime juice
1/2 lb cooked spaghetti
    noodles

Directions

Melt butter in a medium stockpot. Thinly slice onion and mushrooms, sauté until just soft. Add mussels and stir until they start to pop open. 2 to 3 minutes. Throw out any mussels that do not open. Add water and chicken soup base in the pot and stir about a minute. Peel hard-boiled eggs. Grate ginger, add remaining ingredients except for your pasta. Bring to a simmer add pasta and simmer 3 to 4 minutes to make sure pasta is warm. I serve this in wide shallow bowls slice each egg in half and place in a bowl of soup.

Food For The Family Soul
Call Your Mother in Law to make Asian Green Beans. Call Your Sister to make Almond Coconut Cookies

Creamy Chicken Tortilla Soup
HOMESTYLE * KETO * NUT FREE

Carbs 13.1g Protein 6.1g

Mexican nights are a favorite around the house. I came up with this creamy chicken tortilla one night, and it became a massive hit with my husband. It's easy to make and super satisfying. Really this is a home-style soup with all its creaminess.

Makes 6 Servings

2 chicken breasts cooked and shredded
2 cups Mexican shredded cheese
1 1/2 cups sour cream
1 can organic cream of mushroom soup
1 cup chicken bone broth
2 tsp taco seasoning
1/2 tsp dried cilantro
1 cup riced cauliflower

Directions

Place all ingredients in a soup pot except for the cauliflower. Bring to a low simmer stirring frequently until all the cheese is melted and everything is incorporated. Stir in cauliflower and cook for 5 minutes. Its ready. I leave a bit of firmness to the cauliflower, if you cook it to much it will get mushy. Garnish with some tortilla chips if you like.

Food For The Family Soul
Call Your Mother in Law to make Mexican Roulade

Butternut Squash Curry Soup

Carbs 17.1g Protein 5.9g

This is a favorite soup of my daughter and I. I make this soup probably once a week, it is an all around feel better soup. There is just enough ginger and curry to help your throat or your stomach if you're feeling a little off. We often top this soup with some cubed avocado.

Makes 6 Servings

1 1/2 tbsp of coconut oil
1/2 medium onion chopped
4 cloves garlic chopped
1 1/2 tsp minced ginger root
2 tbsp curry powder
2 1/2 cups chicken bone broth
12 oz frozen butternut squash
2 medium carrots peeled and chopped
1 small sweet potato peeled and chopped
1 cup unsweetened coconut milk
1 tbsp lime juice
salt to taste

Directions

In a soup pot place the coconut oil over medium heat. Add onion and sauté for about five minutes. Add garlic, ginger, and curry powder continue to sauté for another 2 minutes. Add chicken bone broth, butternut squash, carrots, and sweet potato bring to a simmer, reduce heat and let cook covered for 40 minutes. Stir occasionally. Turn off heat and transfer soup into a high-speed blender and blend until smooth. Add coconut milk. Blend the soup until very smooth. Return soup to the stockpot. Add lime juice. Heat soup and serve.

*Food For The Family Soul
Call Your Mother in Law to
make Cheesy Buns.*

Brunch My Favorite Meal

Low Carb Hash

Carbs 6.8g Protein 0.8g

This is something I make on the weekends, it takes the place of potato hash. I love Brunch it's one of the best meals of

Makes 4 Servings

2 tbsp butter divided
1/2 cup chopped red
   onion
3 sweet mini peppers
   chopped
1 clove garlic minced
2 cups riced cauliflower
salt and pepper to taste

Directions

Melt 1 tablespoon of butter in skillet add onions and sauté. Once onions are soft add peppers and garlic, sauté for one minute add riced cauliflower and the remaining butter. Cook stirring until cauliflower is tender add salt and pepper to taste. I like a lot of pepper in this.

the whole week. Brunch in the one meal that you can serve anything.

Food For The Family Soul
Call Your Mother in Law to make
Italian Country Eggs.

Basic Breakfast

Carbs 17.8g Protein 21.4g

I was asked to put some of my simple everyday recipes into the book. This is my go-to breakfast to get my day started. I have one serving here, you can double this; however many times you want, Sometimes I make two one for me and one for my daughter. Most days it is just me.

Makes 1 serving

1/2 tbsp butter
2 eggs
1 avocado
2 tbsp feta cheese
2 tbsp salsa

Directions

Melt butter over medium-low heat in a small skillet. Crack each egg and gently slide into skillet one at a time. Cook eggs until whites are cooked through and yellows are getting thicker. Use a spatula to gently flip your eggs over and cook until the desired doneness. I like mine over easy. My yolk is still runny. Cut avocado in half and remove the pit. Remove the fruit from the skin and slice. Place eggs on top of avocado and sprinkle with feta and salsa. Enjoy!

Food For The Family Soul
Call Your Mother in Law to make
Chocolate Chip Power Muffins

Pre-Work Out Breakfast

Carbs 29g Protein 7g

I love how simple and fresh these are. If you are a T1D watch the size of your apple, it can take a long time to work it off if your apple is too big. If your apple is large, just use half your apple and save the other half for later. If you want to make your own almond butter, the recipe is in Tasty Toppers. These are easy to whip up for a crowd before a walk or group exercise. I also like them for a snack.

Makes 1 serving

Directions

1 honey crisp Apple
2 tbsp no sugar
added almond butter

Slice your apple into 4 sections and remove core and seeds. Top each section with 1/4 of your almond butter. Enjoy.

Food For The Family Soul
Call Your Mother in Law to make
Egg Cups.

Spiced Sweet Potatoes With Smashed Egg

GLUTEN FREE * KETO * MEDITERRANEAN * NUT FREE
PALEO

Carbs 10.2g Protein 9.9g

This is a breakfast you can make for a crowd without making a big mess in the kitchen. It warm comfort. My daughter and I love this one on the weekends.

Makes 8 Servings

1 1/2 tbsp butter room temperature
1 tsp salt
1 tsp paprika
1/4 tsp ground cumin
1/4 tsp granulated garlic
1/4 tsp ancho powder
1/4 tsp thyme`
2 large sweet potatoes washed and cut into quarters
8 eggs
4 oz goat cheese

Preheat oven to 400 degrees. Mix spices and butter together and put to the side. Crosshatch the flesh side of the sweet potato only about an inch deep, not all the way to the skin. Cover each sweet potato with spiced butter. On a baking sheet, place each sweet potato cut side down. Bake for 15 mins. Flip potatoes to other side and bake another 10 minutes. Bring a small pot of water to a boil. Gently add eggs to water and boil for 6 1/2 minutes put eggs into an ice bath for 2 minutes. Remove shells from eggs. Plate your sweet potatoes top with one soft boiled egg and break open. Repeat for each serving. Sprinkle each potato with crumbled goat cheese. Serve while warm.

Food For The Family Soul
Call Your Mother in Law to make overnight oats

Banana Bread

Carbs 37.2g Protein 3.6g

I worked on this recipe years ago until I got it right. The
neighborhood kids in Florida were eating
different loaves of banana bread for about a week until I got it
right.

Makes 8 Servings

4 tbsp butter
1 egg
2/3 cup sugar
2 Bananas (very Ripe)
1 1/4 cup flour,
    unbleached
1 tsp baking soda
1/2 tsp Nutmeg
1 tsp Cinnamon
1 1/2 tbsp rum
1 1/2 tsp Vanilla

Directions

Preheat oven 350
Cream Butter, egg and sugar.
Peal banana's and chop add to
mixture and mix until smooth.
Sift dry ingredients and mix
with creamed mixture. Add
Rum and Vanilla thoroughly mix
and bake in a greased loaf pan,
bake 30 to 40 minutes. Serve
sliced and warm plain or with
Irish butter.

Food For The Family Soul
Call Your Mother to Lemon Ricotta Pancakes.
Call your Sister to make Cranberry Orange
Muffins.

Low Carb Pastries

GLUTEN FREE * HOMESTYLE * KETO

Carbs 5.6g Protein 6.6g

I could not help it. This recipe has become so popular I just felt this book was not complete without it. I have tweaked it a few times, and I love how I don't have to feel guilty about them or worry about a post spike in sugar.

Makes 12 Pastries

2 egg whites

Dry ingredients
1 cup almond flour
1 scoop unflavored
   protein powder
1 tbsp coconut sugar
1 tsp baking powder
1 tsp chia seeds
1/2 tsp cinnamon

Wet Ingredients
2 egg yolks
1/2 cup greek yogurt
1 1/2 tbsp melted butter
2 tbsp water
2 tsp vanilla
Extra pat of butter

Cream Cheese
Topping
5 oz cream cheese
1 tbsp coconut sugar
2 tsp vanilla
1tbsp butter melted

Directions

I broke this down to make it simple. Each grouping needs its own bowl. Preheat oven to 350. Beat egg whites to stiff peaks, set to the side. Mix dry ingredients until incorporated. In another bowl mix wet ingredients. Add half a cup of dry mix to wet mix at a time while mixing. Mix until combined together. Using a soft spatula, fold in egg whites to batter 1/3 at a time. Grease your muffin pan with a pat of butter. Using a cookie scoop, place one scoop of batter in each muffin top circle. Mix cream cheese topping together. I warm it in the microwave just a little to make it easier to work with. Place 2 tsp of cream cheese mixture on top of each batter blob. Bake in the oven for about 15 minutes, until edges start to brown. Let cool before lifting out of pan.

Food For The Family Soul
Call Your Mother in law to make some
Berries And Cream

111

Sweet Conversations

Whipped Tiramisu custard

Carbs 11.6g Protein 10.1g

This is a great low carb dessert, Tiramisu richness without all the carbs. Great late night snack, the fat in the recipe helps my sugar stay stable overnight.

Makes 4 Servings

5 eggs
3 tbsp coconut sugar
1 tbsp rum
1/2 tsp instant expresso
1 8oz container
    Mascarpone cheese
1 square of dark bakers
    chocolate

Directions

Place your eggs in a bowl that you can use as a double boiler. Add sugar, Rum and instant expresso, whisk together. Place bowl over boiling water, whisking the entire time. Once eggs double in size remove from heat and let cool. Be careful not to overcook, or they will curdle. Gently fold egg custard with mascarpone. Once incorporated place custard into 4 dishes. Chill for at least an hour before serving. When ready to serve, grate bakers chocolate over each custard. This is truly low guilt dessert. Enjoy.

Food For The Family Soul
Call Your Mother in Law to make Italian Bake

Biscotti

KETO * MEDITERRANEAN * PALEO

Carbs 11.6g Protein 6.1g

I love these twice-baked Italian cookies. They are not meant to be very sweet. Making these early in the morning or even the day before is great for guests staying at your house. They are intended to be served with coffee and dipped.

Makes 12 Servings

2 1/2 cups almond flour
2 tsp cinnamon
1 tsp baking powder
2 tbsp coconut oil
1/4 cup Raw Honey
2 eggs
1 tsp vanilla
1 tsp Grand Marnier

Directions

Pre-heat oven to 350.
Mix dry ingredients together with electric mixer or fork. I have used a fork since I was a kid. Melt coconut oil and mix wet ingredients together. Add dry ingredients. Mix thoroughly. Place parchment paper on a baking sheet. Shape dough into a log that is even and about seven inches long, 3/4 inches high and 4 inches wide. Cook for 20 to 30 minutes until edges start to brown. Take out of oven and cool for 20 to 30 minutes. This step is crucial so that your cookies stay together and don't crumble. Heat oven to 300. Once cookie log is cool slice with a large knife going straight down. Cut into 1/2 to 3/4 inch slices. Gently lay out on parchment paper. Place back in oven and bake on each side 8-10 more minutes. Turn off oven and let cool in oven with the door ajar.

Option: If you want to make them fancy melt some dark chocolate and dip one side in the chocolate. Sprinkle with a dash of sea salt.

Food For The Family Soul
Call Your Mother in Law to make Hot Buttered Coffee

Food For The Family Soul
Call Your Mother in Law to make Spring
Shrimp Spaghetti Squash

Lemon Shortbread Cookie

Carbs 4.5g Protein 2.3g

Shortbread is one of my favorite cookies. I was so excited to work on a low carb recipe for this bite of buttery goodness. When I first started working on this recipe, I used stevia. Using stevia turned out great. Once I started working with coconut sugar, I switched. You could make these with stevia if you want them lower in carb.

Makes 16 cookies

1/2 cup butter softened
3 tbsp coconut sugar
Zest of one lemon
1 tbsp lemon juice
1 tsp vanilla extract
2 1/2 cups almond flour

Directions

Preheat oven 350 degrees Whisk butter and sugar together until light and fluffy. Zest lemon into butter mix, making sure not to include the pith (white part). Add lemon juice and vanilla to mix. Start adding 1/2 cup of almond flour at a time. The batter will be crumbly. I like to use a medium cookie scoop for accuracy in carb count. Recipe makes 16 cookies. Use a half sheet pan lined with parchment paper, place scoops of batter on cookie sheet. Cookies will not spread, so you do not need a lot of space between each cookie. I use a fork to create a cross-hatch pattern and flatten each cookie. Bake cookies in preheated oven for 12-14 minutes until edges turn golden. Place cookie sheet on a cooling rack. Let cookies cool completely.

Ricotta Cheese Cake

KETO * MEDITERRANEAN * PALEO

Carbs 18.3g Protein 12.3g

Cheese, yes, please. I love a simple cheesecake, no need to mess up a perfectly good dessert smothering it with leftover Halloween candy. Do you ever think that? Or is it just me?

Makes 8 Servings

Crust
6 tbsp butter
1 cup almond flour
1 tbsp vanilla
coconut sugar
1 tsp cinnamon

filling
2 cups whole milk Ricotta
3 eggs beaten
1/3 cup Honey
1 tsp vanilla

Directions
Preheat oven to 375
Melt butter and mix with remaining crust ingredients until fully incorporated. Place crust in the bottom of a 7-inch spring form pan. Flatten in the base of the dish so crust is even. Bake crust in oven until one shade darker about 8 to 10 minutes. Let cool completely. Wrap base of pan with foil so the water will not be able to seep in at the edges.

With an electric mixer beat ricotta until fluffy. Mix in vanilla and honey. Gently add eggs one at a time until just incorporated.   Pour filling into cooled crust. Bake in a water bath for 30 mins. Center should still jiggle a little. Let cool, place in refrigerator and chill two hours. Serve chilled.

Food For The Family Soul
Call Your Mother in Law to make some
Spiced Whipped Cream.

Mexican Spiced Chocolate Chip Cookies

Carbs 9.8g Protein 3g

There is this hot chocolate mix that we get at the Latin grocery.
It is my son's favorite we use to serve it at our annual Santa
party in Fl. This warm spicy cocoa inspired these cookies.

Makes 24

8 tbsp softened butter
1/2 cup coconut sugar
2 eggs
2 1/2 cups almond flour
1 tsp baking powder
2 tsp cinnamon
2 tsp vanilla
1/8 tsp ground cloves
1/8 tsp ground nutmeg
1/2 cup chocolate chips
extra dark

Directions
preheat oven to 350 degrees.

Using an electric mixer, cream
butter, and sugar. Add
remaining ingredients, mixing
in the chocolate chips last.
Use a cookie scoop to scoop out
each ball of mix onto a cookie
sheet. Flatten down cookie balls
a little with fingers so that they
are more of an even disk.
Bake about 20 minutes until
golden.

*Food For The Family Soul
Call Your Mother in Law to make some
Mexican Meatball Soup.*

Apple Crumble

Carbs 26.4g Protein 3.2g

Ok so let me tell you how I really feel. I don't like many cooked fruits. Warming perfectly sweet crisp fruit loses its appeal to me. The only crumble or cobbler for that matter I will eat is apple. Don't bring some berry over here. My Apple Crumble is a wonder for its topping, gives all the crunch without the spikes from flour and oats.

Makes 6 servings
5 Granny Smith apples
1 tbsp honey
2 tsp arrowroot
zest of 1 lemon
1 tbsp lemon juice
1 1/2 tsp ground cinnamon
1/2 tsp ground ginger
1/4 tsp nutmeg

topping
1/4 cup butter
3/4 cup chopped pecans
1/2 cup almond flour
1/2 cup unsweetened shaved coconut
1/2 tsp round cinnamon
2 tbsp coconut sugar

Directions
Preheat oven to 350.
Peel, core and slice apples. Each slice should be about a 1/4 inch thick. Toss slices with lemon juice. To keep from browning. Add remaining ingredients for filling and toss with apples. Place in a baking dish.

For topping use room temperature butter and mix all topping ingredients with hands so that it is crumbly. Spread evenly on top of apples. Bake in the oven about 40 minutes.

This is not as sweet as other versions. Add more sugar or honey, remember the addition will increase the carbs.

Food For The Family Soul
Call Your Mother in Law to make
Vanilla Cinnamon Ice Cream

Tasty Toppers

Almond Butter

Carbs 10.7g Protein 10.5g

I buy my almonds in big bags from the wholesale club. When I bring them home, I pour the entire bag on a cookie sheet and roast them in the oven. That way they are ready to snack on, bake with or make almond butter. Cooking them helps you get more nutrition from them.

Makes 10 servings

3 1/2 cups unsalted almonds
1 tbsp coconut oil

Directions

Preheat oven 350
Place almonds on a cookie sheet. Put almonds in the oven for 8 to 10 minutes. Until you smell a nutty aroma.   Cool almonds completely. This is very important. If the almonds are still warm almond butter will not turn out correct. Use a food processor or high-speed blender place coconut oil and then pour in almonds. Blend until you get the desired consistency you want. Chunky to smooth. Store in the refrigerator. I make this each week

Food For The Family Soul
Call Your Mother in Law to make some protein balls with the almond butter you have made.

Magic Green Sauce

Carbs 3.5g Protein 2.1g

This is a go-to sauce. Great for taco night. I love it on taco salad instead of sour cream. It's magic because when put on broccoli kids eat broccoli. Magic!

Makes 10 servings

2 poblano peppers
1 8 oz package of cream
   cheese
1 cup water
4 tbsp butter softened
1 tbsp chicken soup base

Directions

Roast the peppers until the skin is blackened and starting to peel. Don't burn the flesh of the pepper. You can do different ways. You can broil them in the oven or over a gas flame or grill. Turn them frequently. Once they are done place in a ziplock bag or airtight container for 20 mins. Take out of the container and peel the skin off of peppers. Remove stems and seeds. Place flesh of peppers in a food processor or high-speed blender. Add remaining ingredients. Blend until smooth. Warm in a small saucepan on the stove top. Top your foods!!

Food For The Family Soul
Call Your Mother in Law to make some Pulled Pork Tacos.

Gremolata

GLUTEN FREE * HOMESTYLE * KETO * PALEO

Carbs 0.8g Protein 0.2g

I really got hooked on gremolata while in Italy. I just love the fresh taste. Especially love it on top of fresh mozzarella, I can eat it any of time of the day.

Makes 10 servings

1 cup fresh Italian
    parsley chopped
zest of 1 lemon
1 tbsp lemon juice
1/2 cup of olive oil
1 graded clove of garlic
1 tbsp chili pepper paste
1/4 tsp salt

Directions

Place all ingredients in a food processor and pulse until combined.   Put into a glass jar with a lid. Keep in the refrigerator until ready to use.

Food For The Family Soul
Call Your Mother in Law to make Roasted Carrots

132

Spicy Ketchup

Carbs 5.0g Protein 0g

This is so easy it's almost ridiculous to put in here, I was asked to put in some of my super quick recipes. People are always shocked at how much they like my spicy Ketchup. So really it is two ingredients, and it changes depending on the hot sauce I use. Hot sauces with funny names are the best. The current hot sauce I am using is Bayou Pecker Power, my sister in law purchased for me in Louisiana. We love sauces and rubs with funny names. Your carb count can make very a lot depending on what hot sauce you are using, so you need to count the carbs on this one. There is a basic carb count below.

Makes 4 servings
1/4 cup ketchup
1/4 cup hot sauce

Directions
Mix ketchup and hot sauce together until completely incorporated and serve.

Food For The Family Soul
Call Your Mother in Law to make some Home Cut Fries.

Hunter's Sauce

Carbs 5.7g Protein 2.5g

Hunter is my sister in spirit; we have been friends for many years. Hunter has not been cooking for very long. However, she has come up with this sauce that her family loves. They like to put it over mushrooms and Steak.

Makes 6 servings

2 tbsp cornstarch
2 tbsp water
2 cups Heavy
  whipping cream
1/3 cup soy sauce

Directions

Mix cornstarch and water together making sure it is smooth. Set to the side. Mix whipping cream and soy sauce in a pot and bring to a simmer. Add cornstarch and water. Stir until it thickens. Remove from heat and serve.

Food For The Family Soul
Call Your Mother in Law to make some Sautéed Mushrooms

Savory Almonds

GLUTEN FREE * KETO * MEDITERRANEAN * PALEO

Carbs 4.8g Protein 2.1g

I have given up croutons, I love the crunch, so this is my solution for my salads. When I was younger, I use to eat croutons right out of the box, and you can do the same with these.

Makes 16 servings

1 tsp dried Parsley
1 1/2 tsp dried dill
1 tsp granulated garlic
1 tsp granulated onion
3/4 tsp salt
1/4 tsp pepper
1/2 tsp dried chives
1 tbsp powdered
   buttermilk
2 tbsp olive oil

2 cups sliced almonds

Directions

Preheat oven to 300 degrees In a medium bowl place your almonds. In a small bowl, place remaining ingredients and whisk together. Pour mixture over Almonds. Gently toss so that all the almonds are coated evenly. Spread almonds evenly on a cookie sheet. Place in the oven for 20 minutes, stir almonds around on baking sheet every 5 minutes to make sure they don't burn.

Food For The Family Soul
Call Your Mother in Law to make Romaine Wedge
Salad.

139

Horseradish Compound Butter

Carbs 0.8g Protein 0.1g

This is a great topper to mix in with green beans or atop a steak. Make Zesty Chicken Drumsticks. Surprise everyone with your skills and show up at your next dinner with compound butter.

Makes 16 Servings

16 tbsp butter
2 tbsp Horseradish
   Sauce
2 cloves garlic grated
1 tbsp thyme
1 tbsp lemon juice

Directions

The butter needs to be at room temperature. In a medium bowl mix all ingredients together. Make sure everything is fully incorporated. Place butter on parchment paper in the shape of a log, wrap the paper around butter like candy. Twist the ends like you would with candy or party cracker. Place in the freezer for at least one hour.

Food For The Family Soul
Call Your Mother in Law to make Simple pan seared steaks

Who Says They Don't Eat Leftovers

Leftover Brisket Soup

Carbs 10g Protein 25g

In my family leftovers are not popular. So I try to create something new. Soup is always an easy way to use leftover meat. If you make the brisket in this book and have any left, you will enjoy this soup.

Makes 6 Servings

Directions

1+ lbs of leftover
    brisket
3 cups of water
1 cup chopped onion
10 oz mushrooms sliced
2 medium carrots peeled
    and chopped
3 cloves garlic grated
1 Can of Diced tomatoes
1 1/2 tbsp beef soup base
1 tbsp Worcestershire
    Sauce
1 tsp Tarragon
1 tsp thyme

Slice meat into bite size pieces. Place all ingredients in a stock pot. Bring to a boil and reduce to a simmer. Let simmer for 15 mins and Serve.

Food For The Family Soul
Call Your Mother in Law to make Jacked Up
Cauliflower Bread Sticks.

Huevos Rancheros

Carbs 26.2g Protein 22.3g

This is the best use of leftover bean dip and My son's favorite breakfast. I know this will become one of your favorite breakfasts too. The best part of this breakfast is by using the leftovers you can have breakfast ready in a snap.

Makes 1 Serving	Directions
1/2 cup of left over Bean Dip 2 eggs 2 tbsp salsa 1/2 tbsp butter	Warm bean dip in the microwave. I cover it with a paper towel, so it does not splatter. Cook eggs any style. We like them scrambled. If you want your scrambled eggs fluffy, Crack them into a cup and use a whisk to whip them until light and just turning frothy. Cook in egg skillet with melted butter. Serve warmed beans and eggs on a plate together. Use toppings of shredded cheese, salsa, guacamole, or sliced avocados if you like. My son loves them just the way they are with a side of fruit.

Food For The Family Soul
Call Your Mother in Law to make Spiced Chocolate Muffins

Index

broccoli
Broccoli Cauliflower
Chowder   88
Cauliflower Broccoli Bake 75
Nola Soup   91

brussel sprouts
Brussel Sprout Gratin   64
Lemon Piccata sheet pan
dinner   52
Nola Soup   91
Oven Roasted Veggies   81

butter
Apple Crumble   124
Asian Noodle soup   93
Banana Bread   108
Basic Breakfast   103
Brussel Sprout Gratin   64
Crab Stuffed Avocados   68
Horseradish Compound
Butter   140
Huevos Rancheros   146
Italian Chicken With White
Wine Cream Sauce   66
Low Carb Hash   101
Low Carb Pastries   111
Low Carb Shrimp Jambalaya
    46
Lemon Piccata sheet pan
dinner   52
Lemon Shortbread Cookie
    119
Magic Green Sauce   131
Mexican Spiced Chocolate
Chip Cookies   123
Nola Soup   91
Spiced Sweet Potatoes With
Smashed Egg   107
Halibut w/Curried Cream
Sauce   71
Zesty Chicken Drumsticks 56

buttermilk powdered
Savory Almonds   139

butternut squash
Butternut Squash Curry Soup
    97

C

cauliflower
Broccoli Cauliflower
Chowder   88
Cauliflower Broccoli Bake 75
Cauliflower Italian Bread
Sticks   28
Creamy Chicken Tortilla
Soup   95
Low Carb Hash   101
Low Carb Shrimp Jambalaya
    46

capers
Deviled Eggs   24

carrot
Butternut Squash Curry Soup
    97
Leftover Brisket Soup   145
Oven Roasted Veggies   81
Halibut w/Curried Cream
Sauce   71

cayenne Pepper
Brussel Sprout Gratin   64
Crab Stuffed Avocados   68
Kale Chips   33
Spinach Mushroom
Quesadilla   31

celery
Broccoli Cauliflower
Chowder   88
Low Carb Shrimp Jambalaya
    46
Nola Soup   91

chia seeds
Low Carb Pastries   111

chicken
Creamy Chicken Tortilla
Soup   95
Lemon Piccata sheet pan
dinner   52

Italian Chicken With White
    Wine Cream Sauce   66
Zesty Chicken Drumsticks 56

chicken Soup Base

Asian Noodle soup   93
Broccoli Cauliflower
    Chowder   88
Butternut Squash Curry Soup
                             97
Creamy Chicken Tortilla
    Soup   95
French Dip Sandwich   40
Low Carb Shrimp Jambalaya
                             46
Magic Green Sauce   131
Nola Soup   91
Spinach Mushroom
    Quesadilla   31
Stuffed Turkey Breast   60
Halibut w/Curried Cream
    Sauce   71

chili powder

Traditional Chili   44

chives

Crab Dip   35
Savory Almonds   139

cinnamon

Apple Crumble   124
Banana Bread   108
Biscotti   116
Low Carb Pastries   111
Mexican Spiced Chocolate
    Chip Cookies   123

cheese

Basic Breakfast   103
Bean Dip   83
Broccoli Cauliflower
    Chowder   88
Brussel Sprout Gratin   64
Cauliflower Broccoli Bake   75
Cauliflower Italian Bread
    Sticks   28
Crab Dip   35

Creamy Chicken Tortilla
    Soup   95
Italian Chicken With White
    Wine Cream Sauce   66
Kale Chips   33
Spinach Artichoke
    Mushrooms   27
Spinach Mushroom
    Quesadilla   31

cheese, cream

Magic Green Sauce   131

cheese, goat

Spiced Sweet Potatoes With
Smashed Egg   107

cheese, mascarpone

Whipped Tiramisu Custard
                            115

cherry

Low Carb Pastries   111

chocolate

Whipped Tiramisu Custard
                            115

cilantro

Creamy Chicken Tortilla
    Soup   95

cloves

Mexican Spiced Chocolate
    Chip Cookies   123

coconut

Apple Crumble   124

coconut milk

Butternut Squash Curry Soup
                             97

coconut oil

Almond Butter   129
Biscotti   116
Butternut Squash Curry Soup
                             97
Kale Chips   33
Lower Carb Cornbread   77
Spinach Mushroom
    Quesadilla   31

Crab Dip 35
Crab Stuffed Avocados 68
French Dip Sandwich 40
Gremolata 132
Horseradish Compound
    Butter 140
Lemon Piccata sheet pan
    dinner 52
Low Carb Hash 101
Low Carb Shrimp Jambalaya
    46
Nola Soup 91
Savory Almonds 139
Sloppy Joes 49
Spiced Sweet Potatoes With
    Smashed Egg 107
Stuffed Turkey Breast 60
Traditional Chili 44
Uncle Bob's Meatballs 51
Zesty Chicken Drumsticks 56

ginger
Apple Crumble 124
Asian Noodle soup 93
Butternut Squash Curry Soup
    97

goat cheese
Spiced Sweet Potatoes With
    Smashed Egg 107

grand Marnier
Biscotti 116

H

heavy whipping cream
Brussel Sprout Gratin 64
Hunter's Sauce 137
Italian Chicken With White
    Wine Cream Sauce 66
Halibut w/Curried Cream
    Sauce 71

hoisin sauce
Five Spice Salomon 42

honey
Apple Crumble 124

Biscotti 116
Lower Carb Cornbread 77

horseradish
Horseradish Compound
    Butter 140
Zesty Chicken Drumsticks 56

hot sauce
Broccoli Cauliflower
    Chowder 88
Crab dip 35
Low Carb Shrimp Jambalaya
    46
Nola Soup 91
Spicy Ketchup 135

hot sauce, chipotle
Traditional Chili 44

I

italian bread crumbs
Uncle Bob's Meatballs 51

italian Seasoning
Italian Chicken With White
    Wine Cream Sauce 66

K

kale
Kale Chips 33

ketchup
Spicy Ketchup 135

L

lemon juice
Apple Crumble 124
Crab Dip 35
Crab Stuffed Avocados 68
Cuban Steaks 54
Gremolata 132
Horseradish Compound
    Butter 140
Kale Chips 33
Lemon Piccata sheet pan
    dinner 52

154

Bean Dip 83
Crab Stuffed Avocados 68
Creamy Chicken Tortilla
Soup 95

soy sauce
Five Spice Salmon 42
Asian Noodle soup 93
Hunter's Sauce 137

sugar
Banana Bread 108

sugar, coconut
Apple Crumble 124
Lemon Shortbread Cookie
119
Low Carb Pastries 111
Mexican Spiced Chocolate
Chip Cookies 123
Sloppy Joes 49
Whipped Tiramisu Custard
115

sweet potato
Butternut Squash Curry Soup
97
Spiced Sweet Potatoes With
Smashed Egg 107

T

taco seasoning
Creamy Chicken Tortilla
Soup 95

tarragon
Leftover Brisket Soup 145

tequila
Tequila Shrimp 36

tortillas
Spinach Mushroom
Quesadilla 31

tomato
Greek Village Salad 85
Leftover Brisket Soup 145

Oven Roasted Veggies 81

tomato, paste
Sloppy Joes 49

tomato, sauce
Low Carb Shrimp Jambalaya
46
Sloppy Joes 49
Traditional Chili 44

tomato, sun-dried
Crab Stuffed Avocados 68

thyme
Brussel Sprout Gratin 64
Horseradish Compound
Butter 140
Leftover Brisket Soup 145
Low Carb Shrimp Jambalaya
46
Stuffed Turkey Breast 60
Zesty Chicken Drumsticks 56

turkey
Stuffed Turkey Breast 60

turmeric
Broccoli Cauliflower
Chowder 88
Lemon Piccata sheet pan
dinner 52
Stuffed Turkey Breast 60

V

vanilla
Banana Bread 108
Biscotti 116
Lemon Shortbread Cookie
119
Low Carb Pastries 111
Mexican Spiced Chocolate
Chip Cookies 123

vinegar, Balsamic
Spinach Salad with Warm
Dressing 78

vinegar, white
wine

Add A Family Recipe

Add A Family Recipe

Add A Family Recipe